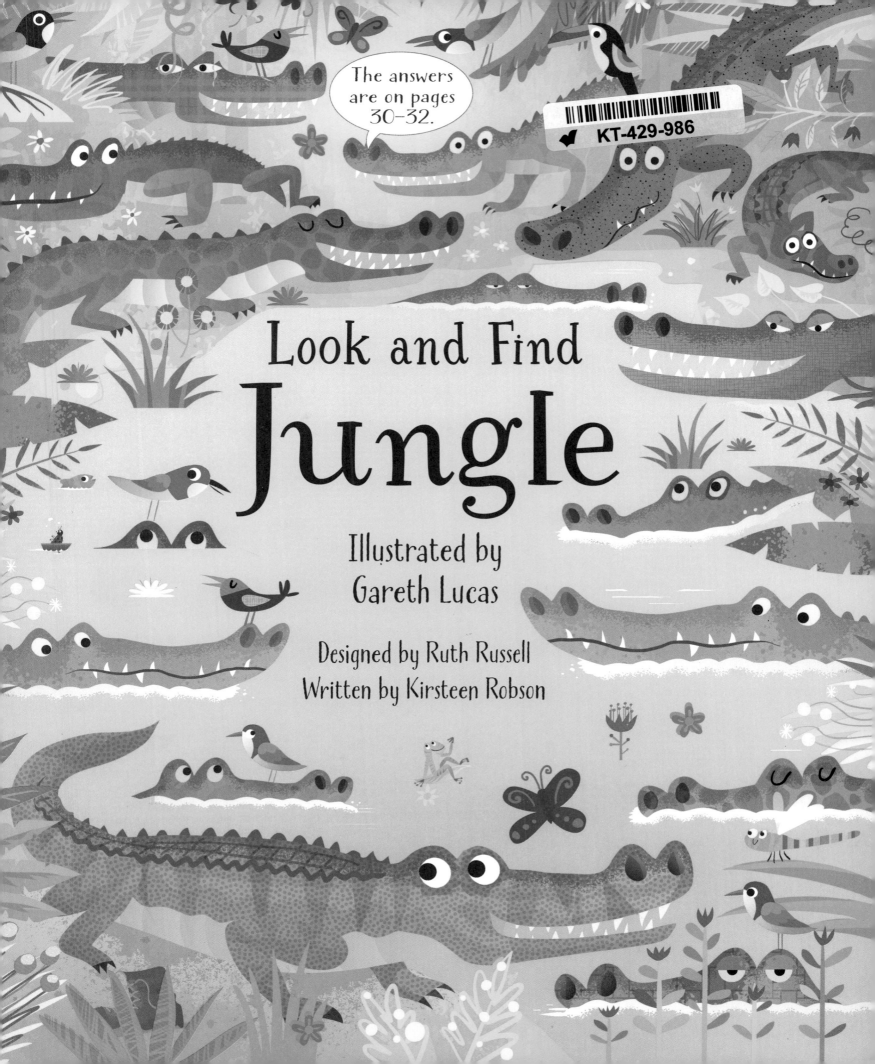

The answers are on pages 30–32.

Look and Find
Jungle

Illustrated by
Gareth Lucas

Designed by Ruth Russell
Written by Kirsteen Robson

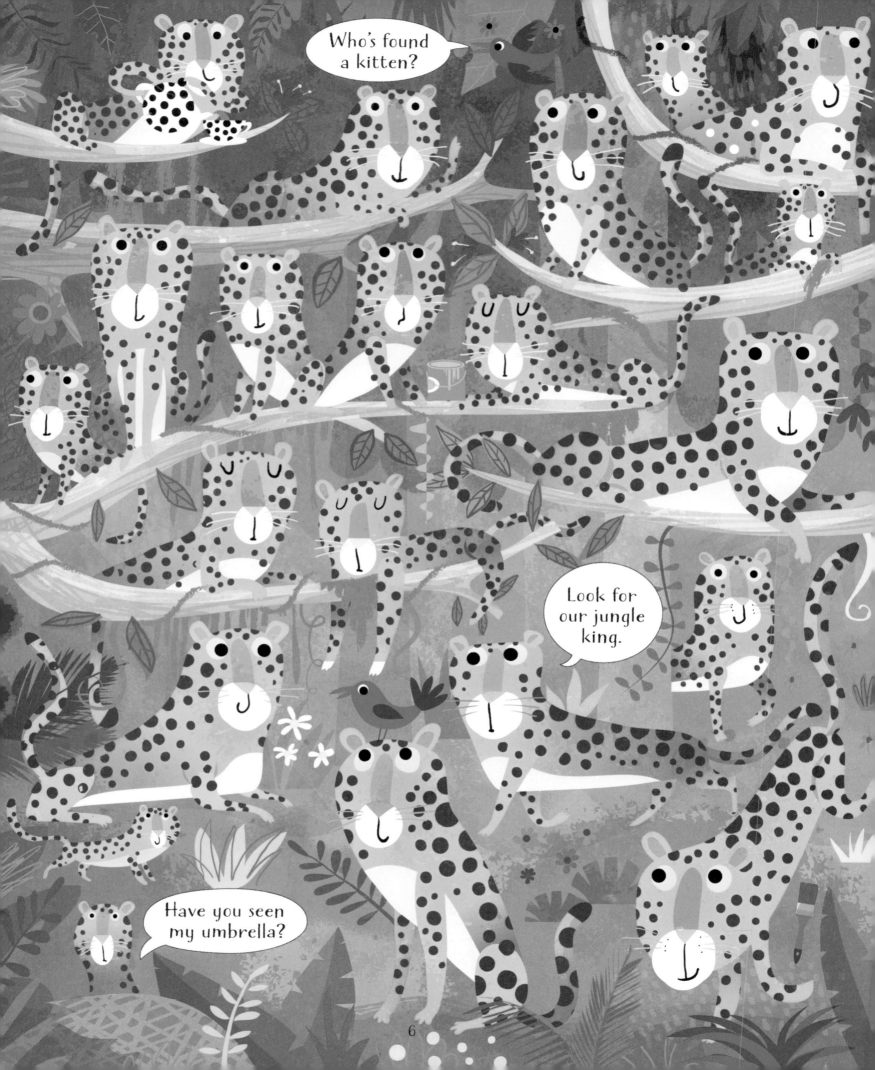

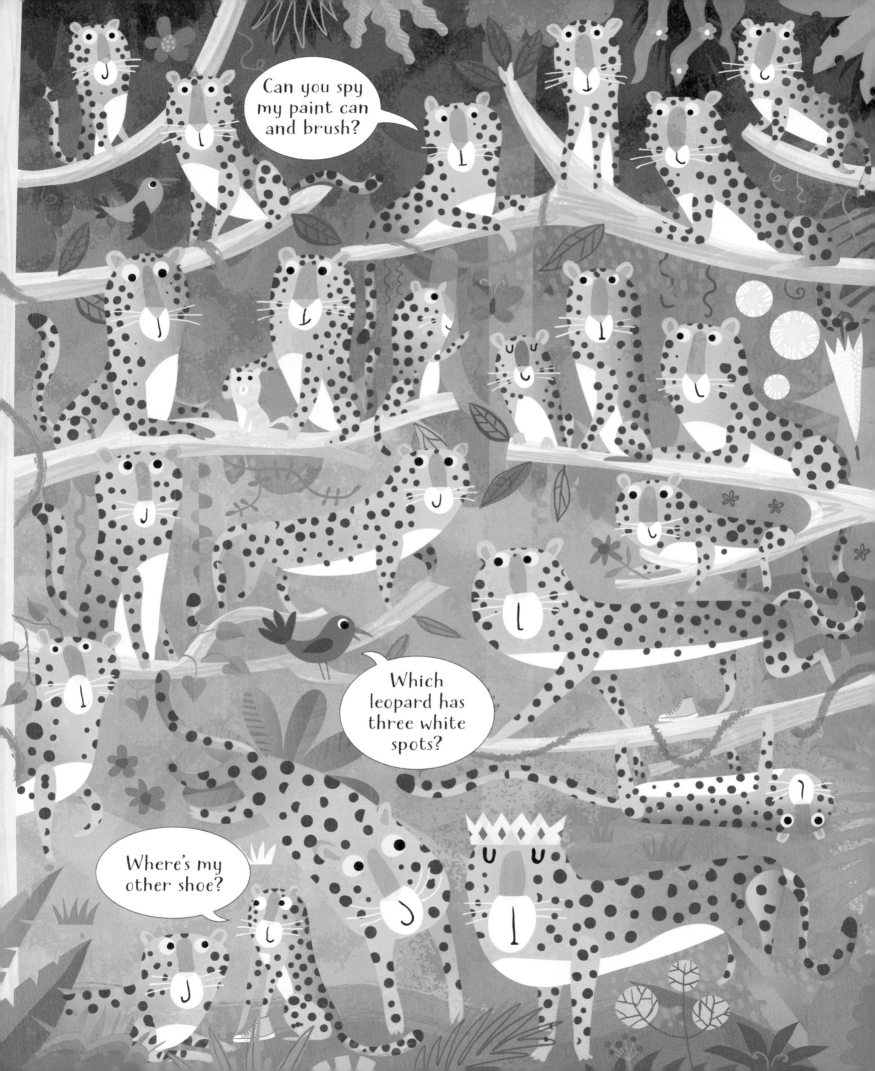

21

27

ANSWERS

The toucan is on page 1.

Cover

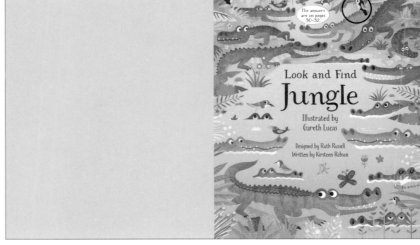

1

There are 5 crocodiles.

2-3

4-5

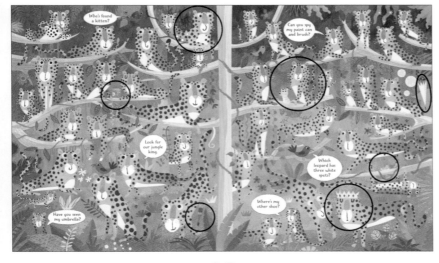

6-7

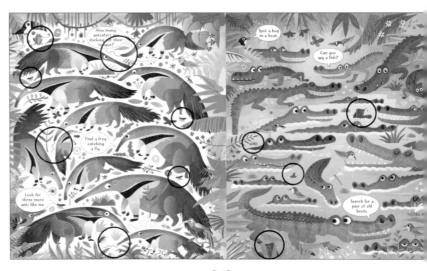

3 anteaters have a sticking-out tongue.

8-9

10-11

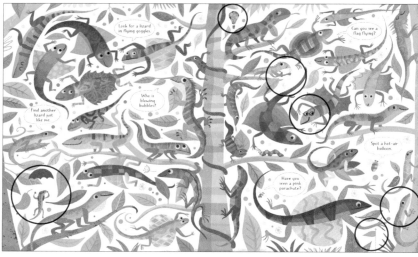

12-13

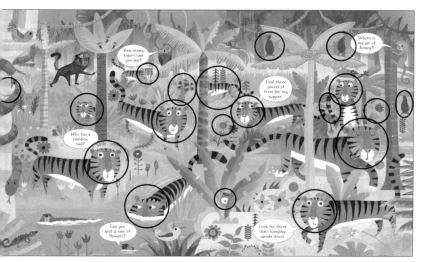

here are 10 tigers.

14-15

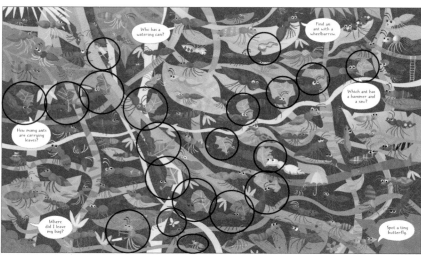

There are 15 leaf-carrying ants.

16-17

ere are 5 birds.

18-19

20-21

31

ANSWERS (continued)

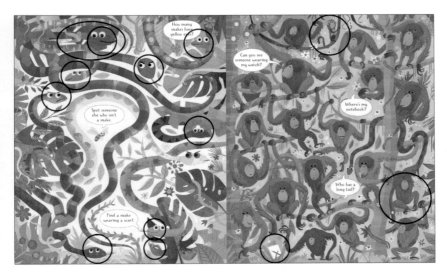

8 snakes have yellow eyes.   22-23

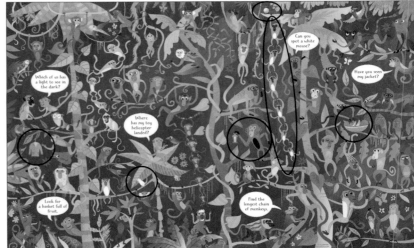

The longest chain has 6 monkeys.   24-25

There are 5 other leaf insects.   26-27

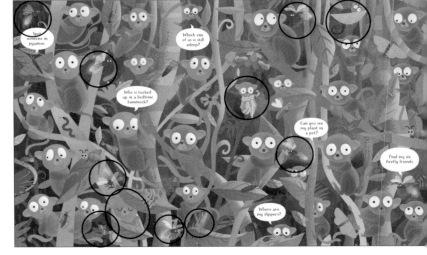

                                             28-29

First published in 2017 by Usborne Publishing Ltd, Usborne House, 83-85 Saffron Hill, London, EC1N 8RT, England. www.usborne.com